CW00666444

Reviews of Life in Verse

Laurie Wilkinson
The Psychy Poet

se

This edition published in Great Britain in 2015 by

MyVoice Publishing

Ubud, Bali

Copyright © Laurie Wilkinson 2015

The right of Laurie Wilkinson to be identified as the author of this work has been asserted by him in accordance with the Copyright, Designs and Patents Act 1988.

All rights reserved. No part of this publication may be reproduced, transmitted, or stored in a retrieval system, in any form or by any means, without permission in writing from the publisher, nor be otherwise circulated in any form of binding or cover other than that in which it is published and without a similar condition being imposed on the subsequent purchaser.

ISBN 978-1-909359-52-9

Cover Photo: The author lost in the Kalahari
Photo by the author.

Acknowledgements

As with my previous two books I would like to thank my family for all their encouragement and support, also my friends, far too numerous to mention all individually.

However I will say a big thanks to Linda M, Anderida Writers Group, especially Liz, in Eastbourne, The 42nd Highland Regiment (1815) and Napoleonic Association re enactment associates who generously bought my first two books!

I must mention my good friend and ex colleague Alison M who has consistently encouraged, fed back ideas and supported me at events.

At my French home site many friends have again generously donated to the charity Help for Heroes, who I support, by book purchases and promotion, Anne & Harry M and Joanne P, in particular in this regard!

If I have unintentionally missed anyone out please accept my apologies and acceptance that many people have kindly helped me complete this third book. MyVoice Publishing again have given me excellent service which I greatly appreciate. My final and biggest thanks is to anyone taking the time to read this book, and my special gratitude to people buying it which ensures my donation to Help for Heroes charity from every sale.

Reviews of Life in Verse

II

Introduction

I have to admit to being somewhat stunned when reflecting back to the publication of my first book, Poetic Views of Life, only 18 months ago last April 2014, and my second book, More Poetic Views of Life being released only seven months later, with both books selling well!

In the ensuing year since last October 2014's publication I have written the further 60+ poems in this book, been interviewed and read my poems on BBC Radio Surrey & Sussex, also Radio DGH Eastbourne where one of my poems is now to be read out weekly too!

I also had a poem of mine reach a National final before being published in The Forward Poetry annual book published November 2014, a feat I am just advised I have also achieved this year as well. If all of this wasn't enough for a "newbie" to publication, I was further flattered and honoured to be awarded Eastbourne's "Resident of the Month" for "literacy and charity (Help for Heroes) achievements!

All amazing but hopefully, in this my third book, I have improved with my continued presentation of mixed themed poems, based on my observations and opinions on life as I see it. The journey continues, please enjoy!

Laurie Wilkinson Bsc (hons) RMN

Contents

Laurie Wilkinson

ROMANCE

Reviews of Life in Verse

Laurie Wilkinson

Feeling Special

When we're together I am somewhere
But lost and nowhere when I'm alone,
For with you I can skip and cartwheel
Though if apart my heart's a stone!

So secretly I'll be your personal ghost
All around, watching with my stare,
I am the out breath, when in you breathe
And I'm the wind that blows your hair.
Thus note the trembling at your sleeve
And feel the itch you cannot scratch,
Because I'm the warm light that shines
Like darkness lit by a match!

When we're together I am somewhere
But lost and nowhere when I'm alone,
For with you I can skip and cartwheel
Though if apart my heart's a stone!

Should you feel sensation at your blouse
Or some finite movement at your skirt,
And heartbeats move to unfelt rhythm
It's just me protecting you from hurt.
Be not afraid when you see a shadow
Or feel a touch, moth like at the ear,
It's just my presence come to love you
And ensure safe passages you steer!

So have no fear of the world around you
Even lightning strikes from above,
For you're safe within an armour
Fashioned by my spirits love.

--ooOoo--

Stupefied

Trembling hands and pounding heart
With every nerve end reeling,
Whenever I see or think of you
I get this strange uncertain feeling.

Drowning in your big round eyes
Drunk and dizzy from your scent,
In a heartbeat I was taken
Not knowing what was meant,
By an apparition of such wonder
With gold clouds over you.
So I stood as before my queen
Unsure of what to say or do.

Blinking eyes and head spinning
I stood stunned beside your throne,
For I had heard of this feeling
But had never thought I'd be alone.
So when my body had recovered
I thought that I should speak,
Though whatever I tried to say
Came out a senseless squeak.

So I had come to fully realise
The meaning of love's dream,
And while I was still shaking
I felt rooted by your beam.

Thus like a nervous child
Going first time into school,
I was stunned awaiting orders
You of course looked so cool.

And with a nod I was called over
With every sinew screaming out,
That for me the war was over
I was lost to you without a doubt!

--ooOoo--

Guiding Light

It took a time to move me
More a nudging than a push,
And when I finally did react
It was quite slow, and not a whoosh.

But steadily laid foundations
Are mostly very strong,
And when we laid our cards out
We saw nothing was wrong.
And so within an understanding
The way was open to proceed.
Thus I felt quite contented
To follow on behind your lead.

So to where it would take us
Be it quite near or very far,
For whatever could be lost
If I followed a guiding star?
To perhaps a unique experience
Or something more to gain,
As I like to have distractions
After which you're not the same.

Nothing ventured, nothing gained
Is a great saying that I love,
And with no preconceived ideas
You may even reach stars above!

--ooOoo--

Laurie Wilkinson

Love to Live

To love is to live
In all things, they say,
As to feel like this
Must enrich every day.

Though some people can't,
Get love past themselves.
And the result of this is
They're left on the shelves.

Others spend their love
All on one single thing,
Which if it goes wrong
Only heartache will bring.

You can love what you do
To give you much pleasure.
So long as it's spread out,
And done in equal measure.

Many folks type of love
Will only bring strife,
Whilst for me it's all simple,
I just love my life!

--ooOoo--

Beam of Love

In the darkness now I think of you
Though you may be near or far.
And if I saw you would I know,
If you're my missing star?

For it is very hard to find someone
If you don't know how they look.
For I have never seen or met you,
Or found a description in a book.

So maybe that's why in the dark
I fantasise I feel your breath,
Because I'm denied sight or sound
Thus think you're a gift from death.

Though you are not here to touch
And however hard I try to see,
I know you, my mysterious spirit,
Are watching and waiting for me.

In the darkness now I think of you
Though you may be near or far.
So if I saw you how would I know,
If you're my missing star?

Why do I feel your shadowy form
As if you are all around my bed?
So where have you come from,
To be inside my head?

Thus I'm making a request to meet
Whatever time, or in a dream.
Perhaps you'll come and take me
To love by the moons night beam.

For now I know what the truth is,
You're a figment of imagined love,
Someone I met, though didn't see
Who'll be there in the stars above!

--ooOoo--

Mysterious Secrets

What is this empty feeling?
And why does it run so deep?
For I've hardly finished planting
So should not expect to reap.

I can talk to other people
Who tell me what they do,
But though they all seem very nice
I just want to talk with you!

You've told me all about yourself
How you live just for the day,
What you do, things you wear
And your very different way.

You told me private secrets
Your very personal style,
So I feel very close up
Instead of my long mile.

You said you were very open,
Your heart's upon your sleeve.
So when I cannot contact you
My heart begins to grieve.

But how is all this happening?
For I am not a virgin youth,
You say that it's a master plan.
So must I wait to see the proof ?

--ooOoo--

Care Waves

Grasping hands that cannot reach
Adoring eyes that never see,
The object that escapes them
As if it wasn't meant to be.

Racing heartbeats are not felt
Loving words lost in the winds,
It's as if nothing can connect
And all love lines it rescinds.

A butterfly can skip out to sea
And birds can fly in the air,
But shipwrecked feelings stall
Compounding their despair,
Of shouted words of silence
That causes a hurting pang,
When the silent words return
Like some manic boomerang.

So dreams can be an answer
No one is forbidden those,
But if a loving sight appears
It just as quickly goes.

A silent conspiracy mocks you
And makes your insides grate,
For even if you start to win
You realise that it's too late!

But a determined love will seek
To overcome and conquer all,
Obstacles that are in its way
Like a demolished Berlin wall.

--ooOoo--

Wish

I wish that I could touch you,
Feel the texture of your skin,
Trace the contours of your body
And see where curves slope in.

I wish that I could caress you
See your reaction to a kiss,
Placed in all your special places
It would be a tragedy to miss.

I wish that I could hold you
Closer if you were inclined,
To run my warm soft touches
Where a woman is defined!

--ooOoo--

Quick Decision

You are new upon my scene
I only recent for you too,
So why a special connection
Without a touch or view?

A photo can project an image
But how authentic is the shot?
And can I trust my instinct
To be the truth or not?

Yes I can get your opinions
That helps me to understand,
But I always like to rely
On the sensations of my hand.

So I would like to feel some
Vibes from perhaps a dance,
For any caress or stroking
Is more reliable than a glance.

Sensations of any nearness
With an appropriate soft touch,
Can bridge any miles in distance
Also telling you so much!

Kind words and sense of mischief
Will bring emotions into play,
And a gentle subtle teasing
Encourages folks to stay.

Especially with humour and notes
And lively words I saw,
About cheerful, emotive smiles
And an opened happy door.

But for me there is a warmth
That exudes without lies,
From a fleeting look I had
Confirmed by twinkling eyes!

--ooOoo--

Open Hearted

Dear lady I think you have my best
But why do I fear I failed a test?
I went away and could not call,
But I didn't want that at all.

You taught me to be open hearted
Though for you I've hardly started,
To say what you have made me feel
For in every nerve you do appeal!

I know I'm a pretty simple soul
But you have made me lose control,
Of thoughts and silly infatuation
Well above senses graduation.

So please forgive my idea of woe
For I value our friendship so.
And what you have shared with me,
I only hope you can truly see
How it has purged my every thought
For on you I'm firmly caught!

--ooOoo--

Lady Mysteries for Love

Mystery lady behind the screen
Most of you I have never seen,
But words and humour bridge the gap
As if I'd used a Sat Nav, or map.

Written words, your opinion expressed
Is one way to judge you best,
And I have seen many of your posts,
So you are known unlike the ghosts
Who haunt some people at your side,
Who are so open they cannot hide.

But there is mystery hanging from you
For I can sense and smell the pall,
And what you give away yourself
Is not anywhere near your all.

Thus I am forced to guess some points
Others like a jigsaw puzzle make,
As to think I have you all worked out
Would be a very big mistake.

Mystery lady behind the screen
Most of you I have never seen,
But words and humour bridge the gap
As if I'd used a Sat nav, or map.

So how could I love a photograph?
Without getting led up the path,
And trying to find out from you
What you'd want me to say or do.
For perhaps you set a net or snare
To surely catch out the unaware,

Laurie Wilkinson

Who take you all on images fed
These crazy suitors, off their head.
No, you need and want a subtle man
With secure promises in the can!

For to know and love a person well
You need to feel them, how they smell,
And this can't be done across air waves
For spoken words and touches saves,
A million written unsaid screeds
That cannot get to all your needs.
So I guess that to know you right
I must caress and hold you tight!

--ooOoo--

Seesaw of the Heart

What makes love affect your heart?
And gets right to the soul,
Putting a smile upon your face
As if you'd scored the greatest goal.

Whether young or old we feel it
This pounding in our veins,
At the sight or thought of love
That's unbridled without reins.
So we soar up to the moon
Or perhaps journey to the stars,
With our stomach's all a flutter
As if returned from Mars!

Oh, of course it can fall apart
And cause hurt that cuts us deep,
But when we've cried and got up
We start again to look and peep,
For another love or partner
To get us back on song.
But of course there is a fear
That it all could go wrong!

Thus round and round in circles
Our spiral of love and tears,
Causing the odd heartache,
But more joy across the years.

--ooOoo--

Laurie Wilkinson

Safe Inside

Loving times, family and friends,
Precious memories shared for you.
Though times may pass and change,
They're safe whatever you may do!

We live close inside our world,
So don't see much else around.
And very little effects us there,
So we sleep so safe and sound.

Then who can see our inner pain?
And take away the hurt and ache,
Of missing people once so close
Each and every move you make.

Thus we must count our blessings
And do this all our living days.
For the memories we treasure,
No one can ever steal away!

--ooOoo--

Local Glory

I really like living in Eastbourne
Though I had visited many times,
Loving the friendly vibes and feelings
With more sun than other UK climes.

Surrounded by the glorious downs
And met in the bays by the sea,
We are protected in our haven
So where else would you want to be?

There is the majesty of Beachy Head
Crowned by the amazing Belle Tout,
And when you climb up to see it
You won't see a more beautiful route!

I must mention though, a sad note
Last July we had a fire on our pier,
And to witness the fire and damage
Caused folk to shed many a tear.

But not a sadness for too long
The restoration of the pier has begun,
So soon it will shine in full glory
With a superb look caught in the sun.

Along the seafront with it's Parades
Flanked by majestic rows of hotels,
You cannot help being content here
As with pride your heart swells.

Take a walk more in the centre
With the many restaurants and bars,
Where you can dine or have a drink
And on warm nights look at the stars.

But one of my greatest appreciations
Is the relaxed, social atmosphere,
So easy to get into a conversation
If just out walking or having a beer.

For the casual ambience of Eastbourne
Takes you back just that bit in time,
And the pace is a small step slower
Whilst hearing church bells chime

Thus we can be proud of our town
With all the joys and treasures it holds,
So join in the fun or just chill out
In contentment as your time unfolds!

--ooOoo--

Reviews of Life in Verse

Laurie Wilkinson

HUMOUR

Reviews of Life in Verse

Laurie Wilkinson

Booze and Two's

It is written that alcohol increases desire
But reduces performance too,
This can be proved on most weekends
When the drunkards roll into view.

Inhibitions and balance both fade
The harder they drink and revel,
With love in the air and emotions high
And skirts raised to panties level,
On young ladies mostly so serene
And always shy of the sexy scrum.
But with lots of drink inside them now
They're more than keen to flash their bum!

Blokes also will feel the effect
As more alcohol lowers their wit.
They think they're great lovers and Romeo's
But in truth most are not even fit.
Though that doesn't stop them at all
Trying to show off all their might,
With them struggling to just stand up
Let alone trying to fight!

Yes alcohol can always take it's toll
Making a fool out of me and you,
For I've never been to bed with an ugly girl
But woken up with quite a few!

--ooOoo--

Syrups

My head is completely bald
Well I shave the bit not dead.
But I could never walk around
With a cheap syrup on my head!

Even the most expensive wig
Won't have anybody fooled,
That it's a healthy head of hair
And that's without it being pulled.

For most syrup of figs are obvious
As to what exactly is up there,
So no colouring or grooming
Can make it look like Barnet Fair.
And I would be more embarrassed
With a bit of carpet on my head,
Than with my bald shining dome
Hidden by a silly cloth instead!

But it's not that you can't notice
A sort of birds nest sitting flat,
That doesn't match or fit right
Like some tatty doorstep mat!

For going bald is quite natural
Most men will at least lose some,
Even the men who kept their hair
Wonder how they didn't succumb!

So most blokes I know are derisive
Of wig wearing guys, so vain,
And our best advice to the "wiggies"
Is to throw your money down the drain!

--ooOoo--

Three's Tease

They say things happen in threes
I've heard that said before,
But if bad things happen with ease
I don't want to play anymore!

For if incidents can easily total two
So are likely to descend on me,
Thus giving me plenty more to do
Without another making it three!

Two's company, three is a crowd,
I heard someone give that advice.
But if making a mistake out loud
I won't want to make it twice.

For I think the saying that two
Is more romantic than a trio,
To get love on with me and you
Only needs one more Taurus or Leo.
But if we can make our love sane
I'm told that we can make another,
Which brings us back to the start again,
Now three with a new sister or brother.

Though if big trouble comes along
With a need for fight to stay alive,
If up against an angry throng
Your company's better numbering five!

--ooOoo--

Fitness Coach

A lot of people are getting bigger
Whatever the cause it's true,
On a train, bus or even a plane
There's less seating room for you!

Our cars are larger now as well
To carry massive folks about,
For to drive, or get in small cars
Many just wouldn't have a shout.
So when buying you must think
Of size, as much as the cash deal.
Whilst the money is important
Can you squeeze behind the wheel?

Of course these mini social tanks
Require a lot more traffic room,
And in a country that seems to shrink
It can only spell road doom.
For most people now won't walk
To get to their chosen destination,
And with bigger diets and less exercise
This is a lethal combination.

For now this vicious circle of life
Will only lead to earlier fates,
For these bigger cars, carry bigger folks
Who are now much heavier weights!

--ooOoo--

Laurie Wilkinson

The Witch

The witch flew on her flightpath
When her bra all turned to dust.
It didn't affect her flying
But it played havoc with her bust!

She had to make an instant landing
As she looked a grisly sight.
So tied one boob up to the left
And swung the other to her right

Then cursing her ample bosom
That dropped down to her crutch,
She reflected on the saying
More than a mouthful is too much!

--ooOoo--

Bears Bath Fun

Ted and Beth are full of fun
Happy bears and keen to laugh,
And one of their special joys
Is in a massive soapy bath.

With water sloshing everywhere
As the bath fills to the top,
Both laughing until they hurt
And their fur soaked as a mop.

Then Beth gives out a cry
As her paw's caught in the plug,
But again screams in surprise
As Ted frees her with a tug!

And so the bears fun continues
With the floor wet as it can be,
But their splashing just goes on
As if swimming in the sea.

Ted's got his toy boat in the tub
And Beth has her rubber duck,
But alas now their play fun
Is about to run out of luck.

For their big watery puddles
Are dripping through the floor,
But the bears still don't know it
Until a loud voice at the door,
Says "just what are you doing?"
An angry dad asks of the bears
Saying that all their splashing
Has made water leak downstairs!

So with a mop each in their paws
And a strong demand to sort it out,
Ted and Beth are now deflated
But will continue to muck about!

--ooOoo--

Have Another Beer

The weather is not great
And through the rain we peer,
It is getting us all down
So have another beer.

We want to drive away
But roads are blocked I hear,
There are far too many cars
So lets have another beer.

A trip up to the shops
To join the thronging crowd,
And mad folks with their trolleys
Make you want to curse aloud!
So you stay at home to book
A holiday, not too dear,
But the internet is down
Best to have another beer.

Then you're on the phone
Many options now to choose,
It's enough to drive you mad
And go back on the booze.
They say you're in a queue
But your turn is nowhere near,
I can't be doing this
So I'll have another beer.

Thus there's so many things
In life to drive you mad,
So have another beer then
You just wont feel so bad!

--ooOoo--

Laurie Wilkinson

Bump Hump

Nothing is more certain sure
To give me the real "mint lump,"
Than getting bounced and rattled
By an oversized speed bump!

They seem now to have multiplied
And spread as weeds on a lawn,
So however you try to avoid them
Your chances are quite forlorn.
Large ones and some wide types
Even the narrow little bars,
No matter how you cross them
They ensure each muscle jars!

Yes I know that they're for safety
And to slow fast drivers down,
But they bunch the traffic up too
So you will always get the clown,
Who tries to miss them out,
Swerving on your side of the road
As if some right of free passage
Was just on him bestowed.

So we're lumbered with these bumps
Which seem as big as hills,
That crash you down the other side
Just like a rollercoaster's thrills.
For whatever technique you try
To negotiate these barricades,
Driving very slowly or diagonally
Your frustration just cascades.

So accept them as we must
For they are surely here to stay,
Or just seek diversions round them
That may take forever and a day!

--ooOoo--

Laurie Wilkinson

Zipping Up

Zip fasteners are so amazing
They have you done up in a trice,
But if they don't line up right
You may be trying more than twice.
Because like little things at times
They won't work and "get your goat",
So you could be idly standing there
Pulling angrily at your coat!

For zips can catch inner linings
Or side material of your clothes,
And unless you zip up correctly
Your frustration and anger shows,
With this aggravating small device
That slides up and down like grease,
Or leaves you baffled and fuming
As you lose your inner peace!

But for men though, there is danger
When they're zipping up their fly.
They must ensure all is tucked in,
Or they will give a piercing cry.
For nothing is so extremely painful
And can make your eyeballs whip,
If any stray bit of hair or tackle
Gets caught up in the zip!

So now we have seen both sides
Of the quick and neat zip slider,
That's so easy to make all secure
So clothes won't gape open any wider.
But we must ensure we zip up right
With fasteners lined up with care,
And reduce any risk of it snagging
To save clothes from wear and tear!

--ooOoo--

Laurie Wilkinson

Trolley Folly

Some people walk slow, others fast
A few may have no choice,
But let them have a shopping trolley
And it becomes their own Rolls Royce!
So like the old fairground ride
With banging, crashing, bumper cars,
Pushing at their precious trolley
Their heads among the stars.

It's my box of space, they seem to say
When clearly getting in the way,
But it has to be the greatest sin
If you should move their trolley in,
And a protective glare is hurled at you
Don't touch my trolley whatever you do.
For if across an aisle like a barricade
It's your fault, and the move you made!

But worse, oh so much worse than this
Is the one, who cannot push or steer,
As you've no chance of avoiding them
However much you try to keep clear.
For with eyes glued on a mobile phone
Or an "oldie" trying to read their list,
It will be more by luck than judgement
That your flesh they've barely missed!

So some will push slow, others fast
But you have no chance of getting past,
For with shopping done, or not yet started
Unlike the Red Sea, they wont be parted
From the trolley front or even behind,
So it's like watching them walking blind.
But the biggest scare and for cover I dive
Is seeing them get in a car and drive!

--ooOoo--

Laurie Wilkinson

Coughs and Colds

Coughs and colds will drive us mad
And surely catch us on the run,
For in winter, summer, rain or dry
They're sure to stop and spoil our fun.

A streaming cold and sneezes too
Will turn your nose into a beetroot,
And bleary eyes and banging head
Tells you that you have a real brute.

Coughing up when you try to breathe
And unable to speak clearly any more,
Are symptoms of the dreaded cough
With each hack painfully sore!

These nasty bugs will lay you low
Whatever relief you try to pursue,
A common cold the girls call it
But to most men it's a "man flu".

Coughs and colds will drive us mad
And surely catch us on the run,
For in winter, summer, rain or dry
They're sure to stop and spoil our fun.

So tickling cough and running nose
Will make you feel a bit like a leper,
And episodes of your sneezes
Seems as if you've snorted pepper!

So don't be dismayed about feeling bad
With watery eyes and head like glue,
For though small consolation that it is
Surely everyone will catch it too!

--ooOoo--

39

Full Bodied

I like Anne Marie serving the bar at The Heron
For sometimes she will have me "in fits",
Where she describes watching "reality" t v
And what people will do with their bits!

But the best part I like from this "bar gel"
Telling about these people and what they do,
Is that it's not just some great descriptions
We get all the actions and impressions too.
She so likes to watch "Embarrassing Bodies"
With peoples large bellies, backsides and hips,
And then explains just how troubles started
With embellishment of her own cutting quips!

I have learnt how folk cope with a big weight
And all they're problems of using the loo,
But without a "shadows doubt" the best scene
Is when Annie M shows just what they do,
With a lift up of this here, and then that bit
And all difficulties and problems, hard to see.
But Anne M then supplied all the answers
Especially how they have to go for a pee!

So to great expansion I learnt all the sufferings
Of reproduction if it seemed "in the bag",
For as our bar lady then fully explained it
They would have no chance of having a shag!

Thus I left The Heron happy, but much wiser
As to just what you can see and learn on t v,
But I also made myself a very strong promise,
That getting obese wasn't happening to me!

--ooOoo--

Laurie Wilkinson

Nellie and I

Nellie and I met out in Thailand
That I can never quite forget,
Along with other memories
On an island called Phuket.

We had gone to a safari centre
All proceeds to help animals there,
And I was really happy to note
An impressive level of care.
Especially the elephants at risk
All treated nicely and well fed.
With lots of activities to do,
Or be hunted outside instead.

So off on an elephant ride then
We travelled all over the park,
To see the animals at their rest
So no poachers could leave a mark.

Soon it was time for the animal show
The elephants showing what to do,
Like how to play games and football
And coming to meet me and you.

Then it came to the show's highlight
People would lay flat like on a rack,
And an extremely large elephant
Put his foot almost on your back.
Delighted squeals and thumbs up
When punters went up one by one,
As if they were to be squashed
By this animal of many a ton!

Then they called for a volunteer
My wife pushed me to the fore,
To get a real close up of Nellie
Though I wasn't really too sure.

But the staff quickly took over
Saying you sir please lay face up,
Oh joy, I was getting a clear view
But I didn't want to win this cup.

Then the girls had soon taken over
Making me lay flat like on a bunk,
Slipping bananas up my shorts
Nellie would get back with her trunk.
But of course I didn't know this
So that I wasn't thinking too much,
That a banana seeking Nellie
Would trunk grope up my crutch.

Well obviously I was very surprised
As I really didn't have a clue,
That when being pressed to stardom
Just what our big Nellie would do.
So I had to just burst out laughing
At this massive shock of mine,
Not expecting an elephants trunk
Up where the sun wont shine!

--ooOoo--

Guardian Angel

To keep me out of trouble
I have a guardian angel bold,
Who makes sure I toe the line
And do exactly as I'm told.

So I should stay completely safe
And on the straight and narrow track,
For with my lookout and adviser
Someone always has my back,
To ensure that from any problems
I am always free, and safely steered,
As my angel will redirect me
If any wrecking rocks are neared.

Thus I had set out in life
Confident I would commit no crime,
Like falling foul of Albatross
Or talking loudly all the time!
So my conscience would be clear
My character wouldn't have a stain,
And if invited out for dinner
I'd have an invitation back again.

But oh, I did get in some mischief
And in to major problems I did leap
So why didn't my angel protect me?
Because the bugger had fell asleep!

--ooOoo--

Stan

Stan is not the man, but a special horse
Coming from good breeding stock too,
A former star of the show jumping scene
He could be well known to me and you!

But Stan's show performing had to end
When he got a bit older and also lame,
So throughout that glitzy special world
It was regarded a crying shame.

So our Stan just got on with his life
Loving all the attention that he accrued,
From his good nature and party tricks
Especially perfecting how to beg for food.
Mints and carrots being a favourite treat
So to get these he would play around,
Following people about to get his way
And to ensure another stash was found.

Stan is not the man, but a special horse
Coming from good breeding stock too,
A former star of the show jumping scene
He could be well known to me and you!

So in his life Stan's made a super niche
In everyone's heart, and all he meets,
Securing himself maximum comfort
With no shortage of love, or special treats.

--ooOoo--

Laurie Wilkinson

A Growing Problem

It's said that what goes up in the air
Must come back down to earth.
Sadly all that goes in your mouth
Mostly stays to spread your girth.

For you're not the size to miss easily,
If your are eating and drinking tea.
When always seen with food to hand
You say that we just don't understand,
That as a "foodaholic" you must eat
As your pigging out you cannot beat!
So don't you moan, to us one and all
If your clothes are now all too small.

For it's said what goes up in the air
Must come back down to earth.
So sadly what goes in your mouth
Adds directly to your girth!

So in a world where people are fatter
Most large folk say it doesn't matter,
To keep on over eating will be alright
Buying new clothes if others get tight.
But as we get older, bodies get tired
And most obese will have expired.
So before this, with a labouring heart,
You can get around in a mobility cart!

--ooOoo--

45

Can't "Bear" to Lose

Ted and Beth love their football,
And get behind the team they choose
When watching matches on the t v,
But are really grumpy if they lose.

They always pick a team to cheer
Whoever the two clubs that's playing.
No neutrality for either of them now,
For their pick to win they're praying.

Beth will choose her sides to support
By the looks and muscles of the teams,
But Ted goes for soccer skill and class
With the best tactics and schemes.
This is alright and fine of course
Unless their chosen teams oppose,
Then there'll be words and argument
That once so nearly came to blows!

But be assured Ted n Beth won't fight,
Of course like most couples they'll row.
And watching football is a powder keg
So to keep their peace they vow.

They do agree on one team though
Who they really love and cheer loudly,
It's the one their dad, The Psychy Poet
Always supported and watches proudly!

--ooOoo--

REFLECTIVE

Reviews of Life in Verse

Pass or Fail?

Cruel echoes of a dimming past
Will hunt you down before your last
Few moments of this mortal coil,
And free you from a constant toil.

How do we receive these memories?
That seem as thick as forest trees.
Will they break our hearts in two?
Or perhaps restrain our perfect view,
That everything we did was right
Despite the haunting in the night,
And maybe make us fear our end,
The devil's angel soon may send!

Thus looking back across the years
Some of laughter and some of tears,
Will sober up any hazy thought
That in error we were never caught!
For every one of us has failed
However from this truth we sailed.

But if we didn't really seem to win
A valiant try may reduce our sin,
Perhaps absolving us from blame
If to a compromise we came,
To make an attempt to favour all
Even if causing our own downfall.

So the stepping stones of our sorrow
Will soon be healed in the morrow,
Possibly our last fading days alive
While our brain tries to contrive,
A covenant with an unerring test
That despite it all we did our best!

--ooOoo--

Recycle Plant

Zooming round his treadmill
Hammy the hamster went,
It seems he really likes it
For that's how his time is spent.
Though for all his frantic efforts
He doesn't get too far in life,
But is this so much different
From many peoples world of strife?

Rushing off through their day
Crowds of people in a dash,
Getting nowhere, trying hard
To earn that bit of extra cash.
And though their chaotic world
Doesn't have the hamsters bars,
It's really not so different
As getting gridlocked in their cars!

And so in our world of wonder
We can fly to our heart's desire,
But many peoples bland routine
Ensures entrapment in their mire.

Thus in cages without walls
Moaning folk are sat restrained,
With all their thoughts of freedom
Yet no real effort is maintained.
For it's so easy to talk of flight
With feet planted on the ground,
Meaning that no escape or joy
From their boring world is found!

--ooOoo--

Nature of Man

As well as my sardonic observations
And cryptic views of life's things,
I also see nature's wonders
Like beautiful creatures with wings,
Or amazing life all shapes and sizes
Living plants in varied hues,
Filling us with awe and amazement
And our eyes with special views.

Mr Attenborough awakened minds
Before all closed to planet Earth,
So now we can be astounded
At stunning wildlife giving birth,
With expanding growing numbers
Living with and around us.
Some we see and take for granted
Others just live without fuss.

But though I dearly love to see nature
My main interest is the common man,
Who with knowledge, or perhaps none
Is killing our world each way he can!

--ooOoo--

Daze End

Sitting in my favourite chair
In my most comfortable way,
Looking back at hours passed
To reflect how went the day?

Well some go very well
And others not so good,
So in the scheme of life
That must be understood.

But more important than this
Is your dealing with it all,
Smiling with the good days
Should give no cause to fall.
But what about the bad times
That can also arrive too?
Can we get up if knocked down?
May define both me and you!

So how well the day went is crucial
But our responses so much more,
For if you react to adversity
Your life will be more secure,
Than if you just roll over
Bleating about your lack of luck,
So if not standing your own ground
You may regret your lack of pluck!

--ooOoo--

Laurie Wilkinson

Word Search

I have really said some dumb things
And looked back on them since,
So that when I do recall them
It makes me groan and wince.

So now I try hard to rationalise
That what I said then was fine,
But no end of new excuses
Will rescind those words of mine.

Some were said in angry outburst
Others spoken maybe to be smart,
Whatever the reason I said them
Now I don't know where to start.

Of course time changes and confuses
And meanings are different today,
But I cannot rest with this now
No matter what I think or say,
To try and settle in my head
That my actions were alright,
So now I must put my hands up
And concede without a fight.

I have really said some dumb things
And looked back on them since,
So that when I do recall them
It makes me groan and wince.

Therefore I must try to find solace
As I'm no solo refrain.
Just one of the many who spoke,
Without engaging their brain!
--ooOoo--

Happy Moaning

Some people always make you smile
While others drag you down.
For despite all attempts to stay bright
You will leave them with a frown.

So why are some folks so miserable?
Are their lives so unusually drear?
Or is it that they have to moan
To any unfortunate going near?

For if the sun shines on them
The weather is much too hot,
But they complain if it turns cold
And so contented they are not!

But there are many folks you meet
With lives and health so dire,
Yet they are always cheerful
With warm natures like a fire.
Not for them a downturned mouth
And a "poor me" on their lips,
For they have a resolution
And a mask that never slips!

So here we have a telling contrast
Of happy folks, and those who are not.
So some will moan, while others smile,
Whatever grief they've got!

--ooOoo--

Laurie Wilkinson

Poetic Prigs Presume

When is our poetry not poetry?
Apart from decree by a pretentious prig,
Who decides his opinion carries all
Like a judge presiding in his wig!

But away from all his dogma
There are mostly differing views,
For some like to tie up every line
Whilst others rhyme in twos.

Then of course there is prose
That forms up in no special way
And flows about a subject,
With no need at all to stay
Exactly to a point or course,
Or even with a topic theme.
Then leads you across anywhere
As if you were in a dream.

Thus as long as it is a pleasure
Poetry can be anything you choose,
From simple usual rhyming verse
To flyaway words about a muse.

That mine is very down to earth
And modern with a story telling style,
Suits me and many who like it,
Though elitist snobs may rile.
At this usurper who is new
And writes simply so you can see,
The essence of the poems
Which certainly pleases me!

--ooOoo--

An Inside Job

On a night of non stirring air
With anonymous perfection,
That's the time to sit and deal
With deeds that need correction.

For any self doubt or sorrow
And a pain that never goes,
Has to be sorted, or put right,
Or it like a cancer grows.

But running away or hiding
Was not the way to solve,
Problems hid, or still denied
Should that be your resolve.

How could you ever run away
Or leave others all deceived?
When you know for certain sure
You will never be believed.

So best for heartfelt honesty
On that night of non stirring air,
With its anonymous perfection
You must be forced to dare,
To tear off all that armour
Which protects the unseen you,
And come to terms with feelings
That on your inside grew!

--ooOoo--

Laurie Wilkinson

Best of the Best

Let me introduce "thebestofeastbourne"
A consortium of great local deals,
Right across the commerce spectrum
And smart places to go for meals.

From photography and sports to builders
The "best of local" can meet your need,
Or on any request you want to make
You can be sure that they'll succeed!

Some businesses though, may need
A little help to make them known,
So "our Mr Ruddle's" the man for this
For he will see that you are shown,
In the very best of shining lights
To all the consumers here.
So people can buy with a confidence
That their custom is held dear.

Thus your local services are the best
For convenience and value too,
And supporting your community
Is the very best, for me and you!

--ooOoo--

Even Out

The rollercoaster ride of life
Will test us one and all,
Just when you think you've won
That's the very time you'll fall.

So up you get and start again
Sorry, but perhaps much wiser,
To continue on your road again
Having fully cleared your visor.

For it's best to see the road ahead
To ensure no fall or trip,
As without a doubt you will err
If your awareness you let slip.
Gleeful shouts you've got it right
Can only lead to sorrow,
For any complacency in this world
Will bring sadness in the morrow.

The wise man says that if you've won
And sport the victor's crown,
Be modest with people going up
You may meet them coming down!

The rollercoaster ride of life
Will test us one and all,
For just when you think you've won
That's the very time you'll fall.

So take any successes in your stride
And stand proud if you should miss,
For if you have done your very best
No one can give any more than this.

--ooOoo--

Laurie Wilkinson

Ensign John

The 42nd were all lined up
A proud and professional sight,
Major Glen gave an order
When a voice said that's not right,
It's not done at all like that
Called the voice of John Hovell.
He'd been in the army for a time,
And re enacted for years as well.

We all looked round despite the need,
To keep some resemblance of line.
Silence in the ranks the Major bawled,
The order that I gave was fine!
A hush descended on the Forty Second,
You could have heard the bird's song.
I only pointed out, said Ensign John
That the order you gave was wrong!

And so this had gone on over the years
Dear old John had to have his say.
But mainly the only problem with that,
Was if we were lined up on display!

But Ensign John was a gentleman
Rarely known to say a sharp word.
And the same could be said about him,
No moan or resentment of him was heard.
I always found him quick to laugh
Even if the joke was about him,
He'd join in the banter at his expense
Although some of the humour was grim!

Away on our camps, John loved his food
With beer to keep him in good stead.
And whilst our John would never push in,
He'd be first at the food queue's head!

John did always like to have things neat
So he would turn out like a new pin.
And I often got a rebuke from him too,
Saying that my turnout was a sin!
But he did though like my jokes,
And on a special time when in France
I told a joke that had him in fits
So much so, we thought he would dance!

Yes I'm sure that we all miss our John
Now he is no more in our sight.
Thus lined up now I still hear him say,
Sorry Glen, but that's not right!

--ooOoo--

Laurie Wilkinson

Blind Fate

Can you feel without sight or sound?
When you only have black text
To help complete your picture,
So you can be perplexed.

Thus you must look for clues
In the written statements there,
Saying their thoughts on life
And how much they care.

Perhaps you can see a photo
To give some outside view,
But pictures can be staged
And aren't necessarily true.

Can you love without sight or sound?
Only having the written word,
If not, proceed with caution
Or you may make yourself absurd.

For I believe you must meet
Other folks and see their eyes,
As there are not too many people
Whose vision hides their lies!

--ooOoo--

Comings and Goings

We open lots of metaphoric doors
As we journey through our life,
But also closing many too
On those who cause us strife.

For there's happy doors and sad ones
And some possible to leave ajar,
If not needing a decision
Though best view these from afar.

So for me it's like the famous glass
That is half empty or half full,
And people are either in or out
Though some outside may pull,
On a door I shut behind them
Not wanting to be left out.
But once I have removed you
That's it, however much you shout!

For a friend or lover who betrays
Will surely do it all again,
And like the leopard with it's spots
Their treachery will remain.
So if you want to turn your cheek
Don't cry out if you get hit
Whilst trying to forgive their sin
Because they never are quite fit,
To tread the same boards as you
Protesting their lesson has been learned,
Despite all the care you gave them
Your love and respect they spurned!

So never fear having to close a door
For a better one will open wide,
With brighter better people coming
To you, standing gloriously inside!

--ooOoo--

Is it Merry Christmas?

Christmas cheer fills the world
All ready for that special day,
Got to have the greatest meal
For the best ever family day.
Smiling faces beam for the photo
All happy sat round the table.
Well mostly smiling, some just trying,
To look as happy as they're able!

For Christmas isn't all it seems
Despite your spending and the drinking,
And peace on earth, goodwill to men
Isn't really what most are thinking!

It all has to be done, put on a show
Make sure the kids presents are the best,
For when they all return to school
Their parents must pass this test.

Not much cheer in the Christmas crush
Battling each other in the shops,
To get all excesses in good time,
You must pull out all the stops.
Or be deprived of those luxuries
The adverts scream you must buy,
So your greatest day stresses soar
No matter just how hard you try.

For Christmas isn't all it seems
Despite your spending and the drinking,
And peace on earth, goodwill to men
Isn't really what most are thinking!

Greed mentality takes over dwellings
Cramming supplies up to the walls,
As if to withstand some long siege
This one day battle is made for fools
Who succumb to the media demands,
And empty their banks and cash flow.
So after the fuss and waste is done
It's not worth seeing your money go.

But I'm no Scrooge or killjoy at all
I like a booze up too, that I must say,
Though I really can't help thinking
How nice if it was Christmas every day.
And not the seasons bloating scene
With It's pushing and shoving crowd,
Who cannot see that just being nice
All long year round is still allowed!

--ooOoo--

Happy Birthday!

Happy birthday, have a good 'un!
Cheers, well I will do my best,
But then I've always done that
For I am very truly blessed!

I am racking up years, not age'd,
But many like me are no more.
So for that I count my blessings
And I have never been more sure,
That I am a very fortunate man.
I have never been too ill.
Sure I have had my down times,
But most of life I've had a fill!

I have travelled so many places,
Tried the wares on many stalls.
Not left many unturned stones,
Playing games with different balls.
I've seen good and bad in women,
Learning from them, having fun,
Perhaps a couple gave me problems
So then I just got up to run!

Yeah happy birthday mate, enjoy,
This special annual day.
But to me each day's a birthday
And I enjoy them all that way.

I've never had to fight in war,
Deadly illness I have none.
So I really do know it's true
That I'm a very lucky one!

I have a holiday place in France,
Where I live is a pretty sight.
So along with counting blessings
I also know I got things right!

--ooOoo--

Reviews of Life in Verse

Laurie Wilkinson

TRAGEDY

Laurie Wilkinson

TRAGEDY

Reviews of Life in Verse

Laurie Wilkinson

Not That Kind of Time

With stealth and cruelty the years go by
Casting spells on both body and mind,
So that we wither and our frailties form
Thus we realise, time's not that kind.

Our resisting brain cells and lively wit
Dispute any damage is being done,
So you still believe you are fit and well
When in truth you can barely run!
But is it wrong to live a white lie?
You're still young and everything works,
For the real truth will slowly seep in
So that doubts and uncertainty lurks.

Going back over time, you now see it all.
The things you did, or should have tried,
For however much you want to catch up
You can't do this when you've died!

The march of the years won't be stopped
Whatever actions you try to pursue.
For once you did things to kill time,
But that time is now killing you!

With stealth and cruelty the years go by
Casting spells on both body and mind,
So that we wither and our frailties form
Thus we realise, time's not that kind.

They say time and tides wait for no man
Though we can do things as they release,
But do not squander or spoil the years
Or you will lose your inner peace.
So maybe best to make a covenant now
As your body loses all strength and vigour,
For the secret of youth and endless life
Is a solution we are yet to figure!

--ooOoo--

Laurie Wilkinson

Dead Flowers

Dead flowers in a field or vase
Have no more glory to show,
For most had been spectacular
Before their time to go!

Strong, upright in radiant colour
They stood proudly on display,
But now their beauty has gone
Their heads sag with dismay.

Some flowers never get to bloom
And fulfil the promise of a spread,
For a cruel wind or sudden frost
Cuts their emerging beauty dead.

Dead flowers in a field or vase
Have no more glory to show,
For most had been spectacular
Before their time to go!

Sadly humans can be as flowers
With loss of radiance near our end,
Despite the glamour we had once
Health and vigour are a dying trend.
But with those gifts we had our peak
And made choices with the time,
Unlike children or young flowers
Who are cut short in their prime!

--ooOoo--

Days of Tears

Days of tears will come for everyone
But for some will last much longer,
Depending on those choices made
Are you weaker, or lots stronger?

For we're living today, decisions past
When maybe didn't count to ten,
So whether we like it now or not
We must accept life as decided then.
Though possibly in previous times
Those options did seem right,
So now you must live with them
However hard they come to bite!

A wrong lover or chance declined
May seem sad in the here and now,
But reflecting back to decision time
You were so certain of your vow.
Perhaps to be childless did appeal
Rocking to your very own way,
But in days of flowing tears now
Accept your loneliness today.

For days of tears will always come
With regrets, and perhaps sorrow,
So best to count every blessing now
Or you may cry at each tomorrow.

--ooOoo--

Laurie Wilkinson

Footsteps

He is a man of constant sorrow
And no pleasure can he derive,
So he really cannot care less
If he should die now, or survive.

The world he loved has broken
And shattered into many parts,
So the grief he is enduring
Would shred the stoutest hearts.

The career he loved is now over
For you have to be fully fit,
And not pain filled and crippled
Struggling to get along with it.

An unlucky placed size ten boot
On bland ground that looked fine,
Took the life he knew in seconds
With that cruel exploding mine!

It was what these heroes feared
An undiscovered explosive device,
That could rip off skin and limbs
Or cause the supreme sacrifice.
So just how do they do this job?
If wrong moves can be your end
They say you just get on and do it
With your comrades and best friend.

Now our man of constant sorrow
Begins to get on with his life,
With support of all his family
And care from a loving wife,

Who tends his hurt and fears
Like those buried deep inside.
So slowly he starts to fight back
And regain his stubborn pride.

Of course he gets help and aid
Along whatever way he goes,
From excellent support teams
That gives help to our heroes.

Thus now he has a strong lifeline
Helping his family without fuss,
So we should all help him also
Giving thanks, it's him not us!

--ooOoo--

Hide and Seek

The man is forever looking
For something he wont find,
As the object of his search
Is hidden deep within his mind.

For on the surface he is happy
From great times that's been had,
But all the time he searches
And on the inside he is sad.

So for what you ask, is he seeking?
Something very normal you suppose
Probably it's a woman, but no
He has had his share of those.
Some that gave him everything,
Meeting all his hopes and needs.
But still his soul was restless
His brain following more leads!

Is he looking for a fortune?
Perhaps fame is what he desires,
But not with surface contentment
It's only inside he never tires.

So fame and glory do not inspire him
Money or women don't make him glow,
Thus he is condemned to searching
For reasons he can never know!

--ooOoo--

Inner Tears

I have heard that when you cry
Tears are words the heart can't express,
Though whatever the explanation
It is a sign of great distress.

Of course there are tears of joy
And some of laughter in a form,
But none can seem as heartrending
As anguish riding out a storm.

Tears of grief or frustration perhaps
Are streaming down your face,
You should not be ashamed of this
As it's really no disgrace.
For those who cry are often caring
And so let their passions free,
Unlike blank faced stone hearts
Who other people's woes can't see!

We can cry at the world's sadness
Or what it has all done to us,
So some will weep out openly
Others cry with much less fuss.
But however you shed your tears
When pain's too much to bear,
It just proves you have empathy
And that you do, really care.

So pucker up, let yourself go
Express emotions and your views,
For if you cannot manage this
You live a life that has no clues!

--ooOoo--

Laurie Wilkinson

Betrayal of Beliefs

Limping slowly the withered man
Wears an agonised expression,
His many years and heavy heart
Now reap a harvest of depression.

Once when young, so full of hope
He felt he could move a mountain,
Though now in his twilight time
Bitter tears flow like a fountain.

For time will wreak aches and pains
Cruelly on a once strong frame,
Though an inner sorrow's echo
Makes him recognise his shame.
For his firm views and beliefs
Held so unshakeable and strong,
Have mockingly crushed his resolve
When he found that they were wrong!

With betrayals of his sacrifices
Lost to others sins and crimes,
Who in retreat left him to explain
And pay for their sordid times.
For mankind will never squander
Any chance to condemn and curse,
The unfortunate of injustices when
Others wrongdoing is much worse.

Thus our scapegoat must struggle on
Too late in life to make amends,
For the wasted time and indignities
Caused by his so called friends!

--ooOoo--

Change of Heart

Carrying a sad and heavy heart
And with all emotions burning,
You have been badly hurt
Your desires just left yearning.

Believing all would work out well
Whilst preparing for a blessing.
But in a heartbeat it was gone
Leaving you upset and guessing,
Why words said to you,
That were loving, warm and nice.
All disappeared in an instant
Turning hot blood into ice.

What could have now happened?
Causing such a massive shock,
To all of those deepest feelings
Making your whole world rock!

Was it something that was said,
Or an opinion now changed?
But you don't know for sure,
No cross words were exchanged.

So to compound your inner pain
You can only wonder why,
It has fallen all apart?
And now you just want to cry!

--ooOoo--

Laurie Wilkinson

Bomb

An exploding bomb's a blast of energy
Massive reaction to chemical release.
It is stunning as well as shocking
Replacing a hell on earth from peace!

An indiscrimination of violent power
A bomb spews both impact and heat,
With splintering eruption and shock
Making varied traumas hard to treat.
Shock will shatter across a body
And damage the internal organs too.
Causing cuts, infection and major burns,
Ensuring nearby survivors are very few!

Bodies ripped open by metal explosion
As projected fragments kill and maim,
Mental scars that may never heal
Should a shattered body look the same!

So we know the awesome power now
Of violence from an exploding bomb,
Made worse in confined spaces
Where living people love to throng.

Now please try hard to explain to me
The workings of an individual who,
Can callously leave such a device
Knowing the mass slaughter it will do!

--ooOoo--

Witness

An innocent bystander can observe
Many "going outs" and "coming ins,"
And whilst not wanting to be involved
May witness an array of sins!

For we are all spectators of life
Though many with blinkered eyes,
Apart from scenes that involve them
Thus they bask under cloudless skies.
Of course until their sunshine is gone
When they will shout for you and me.
But generally they'll be indifferent
As none are so blind as will not see!

So we can bare witness to our world
Occasionally making comment to seek
Correction or change, but mostly don't,
For if not our problem we're loathe to speak.

Though obviously all the worlds wrongs
Cannot be solved by just one voice
That has witnessed man's injustices,
Though some will make the choice,
To make a growing chorus
So much harder to then ignore,
But for many it's too much trouble
And through contented sleep they snore!

--ooOoo--

Laurie Wilkinson

Mobilecide

Suicide Is intentionally killing yourself
When towards that sad act you slide.
But now we have another way to die,
Unintentionally, and called "mobilecide"

For mobilecide comes from the misuse,
Of your companion, the mobile phone.
With all the latest gadgets and devices
That checks you're in touch and not alone.
The problem with this is very simple,
In that you must look at your screens
At almost continual times and occasions,
To ensure you know what it all means!

There are several forms of mobilecide
And can depend on where you are,
But by far the most certain, lethal way
Is to use your phone and drive a car.

A quick look at it, or maybe make a call
Or perhaps temptation to send a text,
So that your eyes are off your driving
And have no clues to what happens next.
You are not attending to the road
So you swerve to left, or maybe right,
At an oncoming car, maybe a big van
But each could spell the last goodnight!

Of course other people may be involved,
Not fault of theirs they're in the way.
But your averted eyes don't see them
And after you hit them, what do you say?
"Oh God I really didn't mean it"
No intention for this at all.
You got distracted by your phone,
So you killed them and hit the wall.

By walking you are not in the clear
If constantly at your phone you look,
Because the unseen driver who hits you
Was surprised by the chance you took,
A pedestrian without any awareness
Of a highway code you may have read.
For to go blindly cross the road
Ensures you very soon will end up dead!

Thus questions must be asked of the mobile,
Is it for fun, information, or tears.
For giving it attention, and not yourself
Means you won't live many years.

--ooOoo--

Laurie Wilkinson

The Singer not this Song

I didn't make the mistake
Someone else had got it wrong,
So when crashing in regardless
They hit the singer not the song!

For the song was sung by many
A sort of chorus choir collective.
But sadly our "do gooder" got,
The completely wrong perspective.
Because when adding moral sums
It's not so easy to thrive,
So when our errant tried it
They made two plus two make five!

Thus the singer took a hit
That should not have been for him,
But I guess that can be the cost
When someone acts upon a whim.

So the wrongly wounded singer
Turned to look around for aid.
Calling out desperately for justice
Saying an error had been made.
But he couldn't quite believe it,
Reeling stunned back from the frame.
When the verdict came back "guilty"
And that he the singer, was to blame !

--ooOoo--

Wheel I Never

We are such perfect drivers
And so never make mistakes,
But curse the other motorist
On the silly way he overtakes.

Now most modern motor cars
Have robot and computer gain,
But then given to many a driver
Who has horse dung for a brain!

Bright indicators flash and wink
Even in darkness they are shone,
But a shameful waste of time
When morons won't turn them on.
Thus thinking that they're coming
Fast and across your vehicle's cleft,
So you just sit waiting patiently
As they selfishly just turn left!

We are such perfect drivers
And so never make mistakes,
But curse the other motorist
On the silly way he overtakes.

Of course traffic jams will annoy
With cars forced into tight clinches,
Made more stressful by the driver
When two feet he goes and pinches.
Which must reduce his journey time
By small split seconds in the hour,
But the look of his ecstatic joy
In the gridlock soon turns sour!

Driving in the heavy rain and wet
With the car in darkness cloaked,
Our clown with no lights shining
Won't see pedestrians he's soaked.

Oh motor car and the motorist
Not such a blissful match of two,
For some drivers are always lethal
Because of the stupid things they do!
Like getting in a car to drive
With alcohol reducing their skill,
Saying that they're safe and sound
Despite innocent people they'll kill!

--ooOoo--

Yellow Brick Code

The yellow brick road is attractive
And can lead to all your dreams,
But beware what is too easy
It's not always how it seems.
Often leading to more heartache
That you ever felt could befall,
With crushed lives and sadness
And best intentions beyond recall.

So you set off on your journey
With scant care or backward look,
To follow a path to promised wonder
But sadly a wrong turn you took.
No pearly path led to your hopes
Or road to make a life fulfil
With no escape to a crowning glory,
Instead it all just made you ill!

You felt you had all the trump cards
And your win was the certain tip,
But it's always as well to remember
That dreaded slip "twixt cup and lip".
For it's not what you have that's crucial
But your use and mastery of skills,
For it's about the singer, not the song
And how well you learn the drills.

Laurie Wilkinson

No sanctuary can now placate you
From all that chagrins hurt inside,
For however hard you try to twist it
You just gave away your pride.
So best to try now and enjoy the chaos
Brought about by the selfish needs,
Sadly no yellow brick road for you
Only shame for sad, callous deeds.

--ooOoo--

Life's Lottery

Maybe our lifetime is decreed
From the moment we are born,
A length of expectation perhaps
From the way of our first dawn.

We can of course influence this
By the actions of our living,
Many excesses of food and drink
Will not be too forgiving.
Inhaling smoke into your lungs
Wont help your health in any way,
From breathlessness to blocked lungs
Ensure losing years, and not a day!

Fortune will also play a part
With genetics and family traits.
Any premature death of relatives
Often mean the Reaper never waits,
For too long to gather you in
To take to the other side,
Despite your pristine lifestyle
And the depths you took to hide.

Alongside this there is fortitude
Or none, if in the wrong place,
Though not any fault of yours
If called, just go with grace,
Despite only having a short life,
And hardly drinking from your cup.
As go you must if the caller shouts,
Come on in your time is up!

Laurie Wilkinson

So now we can see that life's not fair
With the way our death is sprung,
And the final curtain is tougher still
When the best are called too young!

--ooOoo--

Appendix

Feedback on my poetry recounts that many people like to work out the meanings for themselves and even attach their own personal experiences and thoughts. I think that this is wonderful, but for other people who like to seek my explanations please review my comments below.

As I tend to write spontaneously and often on subjects that have emoted me, most of the themes are self explanatory. The poems in this appendix are less obvious themes, but feel free to add any personalisation as to how the poems are for you individually.

Guiding Light	A surprise friendship
Beam of Love	An unaccepted feeling of love
Care Waves	The Determination of love
Lady Mysteries of Love	On a lady hiding her emotions
The Witch	My caustic response to a cartoon sent to me
Have Another Beer	My facetious thoughts on many things that annoy and aggravate us in life
Full Bodied	True story of hilarious incident in local pub
Nellie and I	Another account of an actual occurrence
Guardian Angel	Old joke and saying of mine if I had "mucked up" something
Stan	Story of a friend's lovely old horse
Pass or Fail	Reflections back on our decisions in life

Recycle Plant	Impotent thoughts and ideas of people to better themselves but lack the courage to try and improve themselves
Nature of Man	Some of my frustrations on how we spoil our wonderful world
Daze End	My reflection on how I dealt with the day
World Search	Recognition that we often speak without too much thought
Happy Moaning	That some people never complain, and others will always moan
Poetic Prigs Presume	My response to a snobby, biased review on the poetry I write
Best of the Best	In praise of local investment and support of our recommended services
Ensign John	Tribute to a lovely historical re enactment friend who recently died
Blind Fate	Beware of online friends and relationships
Is it Merry Christmas	On the hypocrisy and money wasting of the Christmas period
Happy Birthday	How I always have counted my blessings
Not That Kind of Time	Do not waste your life or your time
Dead Flowers	Nothing lasts for ever
Days of Tears	That we live today our decisions made in the past

Footsteps	Tribute to our wounded armed forces that I support , but who are so often forgotten
Hide and Seek	Maybe we will always strive for something more
Inner Tears	Don't be afraid to show your emotions
Betrayal of Beliefs	Heartbreak of reality that perhaps all your views were not all right
Change of Heart	Pain we feel if deceived or let down
Bomb	My anger and contempt of cowardly bombers
Witness	That we should have the courage to speak out against injustice
Mobilecide	A warning on blindly looking at our mobile phones and not on the world around us
The Singer Not This Song	On being badly let down by a person you perceived as a close friend
Wheel I Never	On selfish and dangerous drivers
Yellow Brick Code	Parable like story of betraying any worldly commitments and feelings for a false, fake goal
Life's Lottery	The finite nature of our lives

47926971R00059

Made in the USA
Charleston, SC
19 October 2015